THE
DESIGNING
YOUR LIFE
WORKBOOK

A FRAMEWORK FOR
BUILDING A LIFE YOU CAN *THRIVE IN*

BILL BURNETT & DAVE EVANS

CLARKSON POTTER/PUBLISHERS
NEW YORK

Get the must-have book that has helped
thousands of people change their lives.

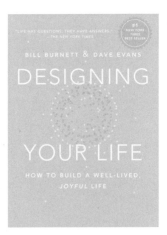

"LIFE HAS QUESTIONS. THEY HAVE ANSWERS."
—*NEW YORK TIMES*

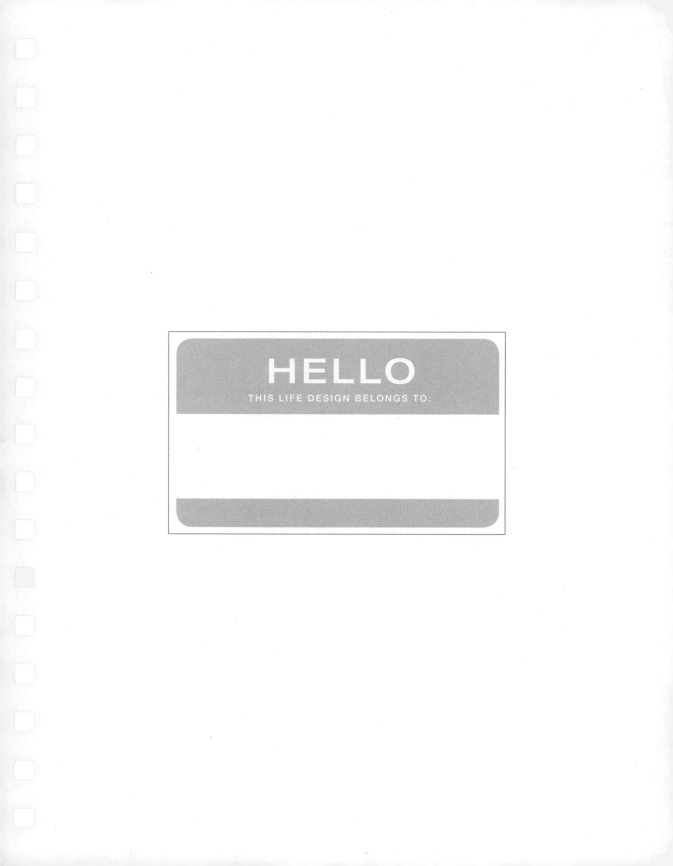

HELLO

THIS LIFE DESIGN BELONGS TO:

Contents

INTRODUCTION

We have all been asked, What do you want to be when you grow up? Whether you are fifteen or fifty, figuring out what you're going to do with your life remains a fundamental challenge. But there's more to it than just having that One True Plan; after all, life is all about growth and change. We can't expect things to always work out the way we think they will. What we need is a process—a design process—for figuring out where we are, what we want, and how we can build our way to a life we love.

We created this workbook to give you a special place for interacting with the tools, questions, and exercises we talk about in our *New York Times* bestselling book, *Designing Your Life*, which is based on the course we offer at Stanford to help students find their first jobs after graduation. The course started a movement, inspiring thousands to make progress on their own goals by approaching life as a designer would a product.

A well-designed life is a life that is generative—it is constantly creative, productive, changing, evolving, and there is always the possibility of surprise.

To think like a designer, you can start by adopting five simple mind-sets. These are your design tools, and with them you can build anything, including a life you love.

Be Curious. Curiosity makes everything new. It invites exploration and makes everything feel like play. Most of all, curiosity is going to help you "get good at being lucky."

Try Stuff. When you have a bias to action, rather than sitting on the bench just thinking about what you are going to do, get in the game and commit to building your way forward. Designers are always trying things and testing them out. They create prototype after prototype, failing often but failing forward, until they find what works and what solves the problem.

Reframe Problems. Thinking about something differently is how designers get unstuck. It also makes sure that we are working on the right problem. Key reframes help you step back, examine your biases, and open up new solution spaces.

Know It's a Process. To think like a designer, you have to understand that life gets messy. For every step forward, it can sometimes seem you are moving two steps back. An important part of the process is letting go—of your first idea and of a good-but-not-great solution.

Ask for Help. This last mind-set of design thinking is perhaps the most important. You are not alone; it takes a team. The best designers know that great design requires radical collaboration.

Whether you're a recent graduate, looking for a transition midcareer, or planning your second act in retirement, this workbook and journal in one will help you identify your interests, revisit your goals, and track your progress. We're here to co-create with you. Think of us as part of your own personal design team. You can use this workbook on its own or turn to it as you make your way through our book or online courses. Whatever you decide, remember there are no wrong answers and we're not grading you. Only you can design your own life.

ACCEPTING WHERE YOU ARE

Let's start where you are. Not where you wish you were or where you think you should be, but right where you are. To do so, we need to break down life into some discrete areas: work, play, love, and health—four things that provide energy and focus for your journey and keep your life running smoothly.

Shade in the gauges on this dashboard from zero to full, then describe what's going on in the spaces below. Is your play gauge at a quarter and your work at full or more? What about love? What about your mental health and spirit? You might ask what we mean by "full." It's up to you! You are the expert on your life; the dashboard gives you a chance to capture your own awareness of what parts of your life are full and less than full.

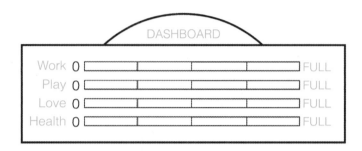

Work:

_____

_____

_____

_____

_____

_____

_____

Play:

_____

_____

_____

_____

_____

_____

_____

Love:

_____

_____

_____

_____

_____

_____

Health:

_____

_____

_____

_____

_____

_____

REFLECT ON WHERE YOU ARE

Let's take a closer look at your dashboard. Write a few
sentences about each of the four areas.

How do you feel about your dashboard gauges?

_____

_____

_____

_____

_____

_____

_____

Do they look balanced or out of balance according to your definitions?

_____

_____

_____

_____

_____

_____

_____

Are any areas full or approaching full? Does that feel good or bad?

_____

_____

_____

_____

_____

_____

_____

Are any areas empty? How do you feel about that?

_____

_____

_____

_____

_____

_____

_____

Which areas could use action, improvement, or innovation?

_____

_____

_____

_____

_____

_____

_____

What obstacles might stand in your way?

_____

_____

_____

_____

_____

_____

_____

What small incremental change can you try out, easily implement, and iterate?

_____

_____

_____

_____

_____

_____

_____

Are there any specific problems you would like to tackle? If so, what are they?

_____

_____

_____

_____

_____

_____

_____

Now it's time to get you pointed in the
right direction for your journey ahead.
For that, you'll need a compass.

· BUILDING YOUR COMPASS

With a good compass guiding you, you have the power to cut deals with yourself. If you can see the connections between who you are, what you believe, and what you are doing, you will know when you are on course, whether there is tension, when you need to make careful compromises, and if you are in need of a major course correction. But to build your compass, you first need to articulate your Workview and your Lifeview.

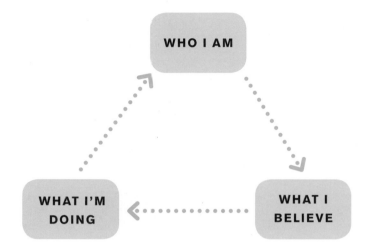

Our goal for your life is rather simple: *coherency*. A coherent life is one lived in such a way that you can clearly connect the dots between the three points illustrated above. As a result, you'll increase your sense of self, create more meaning in your life, and have greater satisfaction. If you can't connect them the way you'd like, there are two ways to address that: (1) you may need to accept a compromise for a while if outside constraints are unmovable presently, or (2) you may be able to identify a few problems that need solving.

AS ALL SAILORS KNOW,
YOU CAN'T SAIL A COURSE
IN ONE STRAIGHT LINE—
YOU TACK ACCORDING
TO WHAT THE WINDS AND
CONDITIONS ALLOW.

Why do you work?

_____

_____

_____

_____

_____

_____

How does work relate to the individual, others, and society?

_____

_____

_____

_____

_____

_____

What defines good or worthwhile work?

_____

_____

_____

_____

_____

_____

What does money have to do with it?

_____

_____

_____

_____

_____

_____

What do experience, growth, and fulfillment have to do with it?

_____

_____

_____

_____

_____

_____

WE MAY ALL WANT THE SAME THINGS—A HEALTHY AND LONG LIFE, WORK WE ENJOY AND THAT MATTERS, LOVING AND MEANINGFUL RELATIONSHIPS, AND A HELL OF A LOT OF FUN ALONG THE WAY—BUT HOW WE THINK WE'LL GET THEM IS VERY DIFFERENT.

DEFINE YOUR LIFEVIEW

Take about thirty minutes to answer the following questions.

What is the meaning or purpose of life?

_____

_____

_____

_____

_____

_____

What is the relationship between the individual and others?

_____

_____

_____

_____

_____

Where do family, country, and the rest of the world fit in?

_____

_____

_____

_____

_____

_____

Is there a higher power, and if so, what impact does this have on your life?

_____

_____

_____

_____

_____

What are the roles of joy, sorrow, justice, injustice, love, peace, and strife in life?

_____

_____

_____

_____

_____

_____

YOUR
TRUE
NORTH

When your Workview and your Lifeview are in harmony with each other, you create a compass that will always lead you to your "true north." With an accurate compass, you'll never stray off course for long. Anytime you're considering a change, pursuing a new role, or wondering what you're doing at a particular job—first stop, check your compass, and orient yourself.

Integrate your Workview and Lifeview by reflecting on the following questions. You may feel you need to edit one or both of your views by going back to pages 14 and 15.

Where do your views on work and life complement one another?

_____

_____

_____

_____

_____

_____

Where do they clash?

_____

_____

_____

_____

_____

_____

Does one drive the other? How?

_____

_____

_____

_____

_____

_____

Now that you have your compass,
it's time to find your way.

THE GOOD TIME JOURNAL

Since there's no single destination in life, you can't put your goal into your GPS and get turn-by-turn directions. What you can do is pay attention to the road signs in front of you and make your best way forward with the tools you have at hand. We call this "wayfinding." The first clues to help you find your way are *engagement* and *energy*. Let's drill down into the particulars of your day to track those clues.

Complete a log of your daily activities, using the journal pages that follow. Note when you are engaged or in flow (see page 48), energized, or bored and what you are doing during those times. Do this daily, or at the very least every few days, for a total of three weeks.

Check out this example from Bill's Good Time Journal:

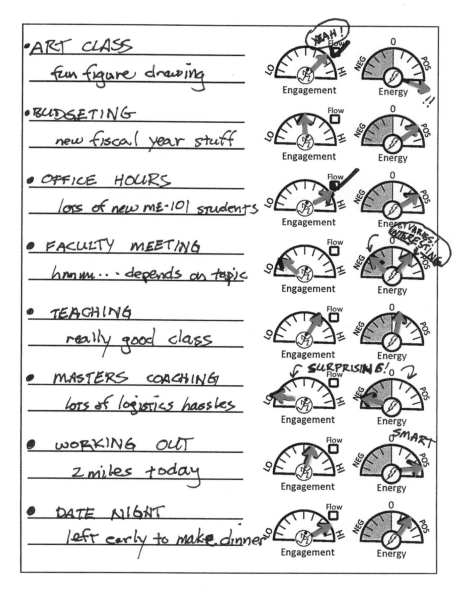

Date: _____

_____

_____

_____

Flow ☐
Engagement   Energy

_____

_____

_____

Flow ☐
Engagement   Energy

_____

_____

_____

Flow ☐
Engagement   Energy

_____

_____

_____

Flow ☐
Engagement   Energy

_____

_____

_____

Flow ☐
Engagement   Energy

_____

_____

_____

Flow ☐
Engagement   Energy

_____

_____

_____

Flow ☐
Engagement   Energy

_____

_____

_____

Flow ☐
Engagement   Energy

_____

_____

Engagement   Energy

_____

_____

Engagement   Energy

_____

_____

Engagement   Energy

_____

_____

Engagement   Energy

_____

_____

Engagement   Energy

_____

_____

Engagement   Energy

_____

_____

Engagement   Energy

_____

_____

Engagement   Energy

CATCH YOURSELF

in the act of having a

GOOD TIME.

Flow ☐
LO ⌒ HI
Engagement

0
NEG POS
Energy

Flow ☐
LO ⌒ HI
Engagement

0
NEG POS
Energy

Flow ☐
LO ⌒ HI
Engagement

0
NEG POS
Energy

Flow ☐
LO ⌒ HI
Engagement

0
NEG POS
Energy

Flow ☐
LO ⌒ HI
Engagement

0
NEG POS
Energy

Flow ☐
LO ⌒ HI
Engagement

0
NEG POS
Energy

Flow ☐
LO ⌒ HI
Engagement

0
NEG POS
Energy

Flow ☐
LO ⌒ HI
Engagement

0
NEG POS
Energy

Date: _____

Engagement   Energy

Engagement   Energy

Engagement   Energy

Engagement   Energy

Engagement   Energy

Engagement   Energy

Engagement   Energy

Engagement   Energy

Flow ☐
LO | HI
Engagement

0
NEG | POS
Energy

Flow ☐
LO | HI
Engagement

0
NEG | POS
Energy

Flow ☐
LO | HI
Engagement

0
NEG | POS
Energy

Flow ☐
LO | HI
Engagement

0
NEG | POS
Energy

Flow ☐
LO | HI
Engagement

0
NEG | POS
Energy

Flow ☐
LO | HI
Engagement

0
NEG | POS
Energy

Flow ☐
LO | HI
Engagement

0
NEG | POS
Energy

Flow ☐
LO | HI
Engagement

0
NEG | POS
Energy

Date: _____

Engagement   Energy

Flow

LO — HI   NEG — 0 — POS

Engagement   Energy

Engagement   Energy

Engagement   Energy

Engagement   Energy

Engagement   Energy

Engagement   Energy

Engagement   Energy

Date: _____

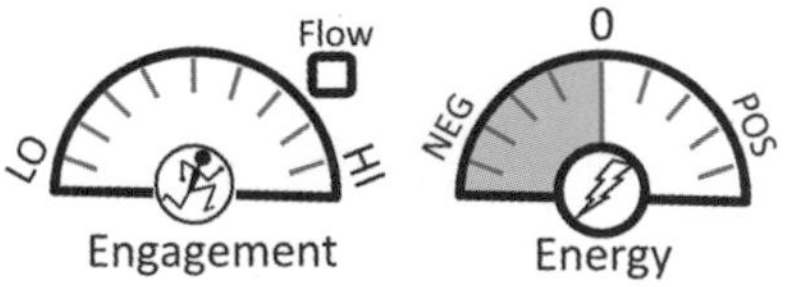

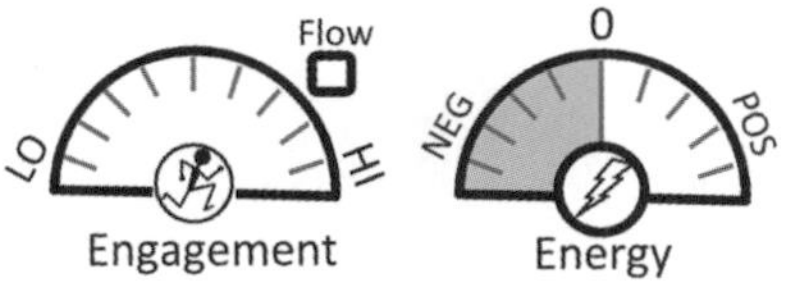

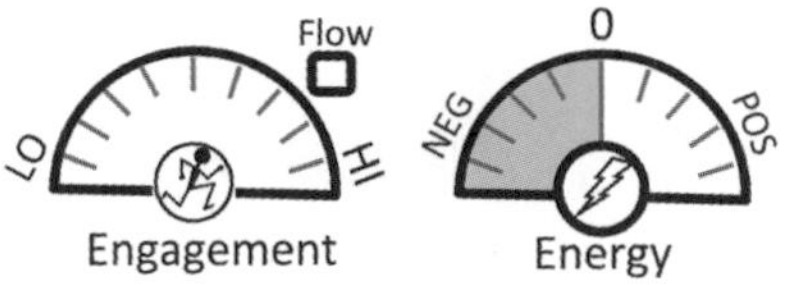

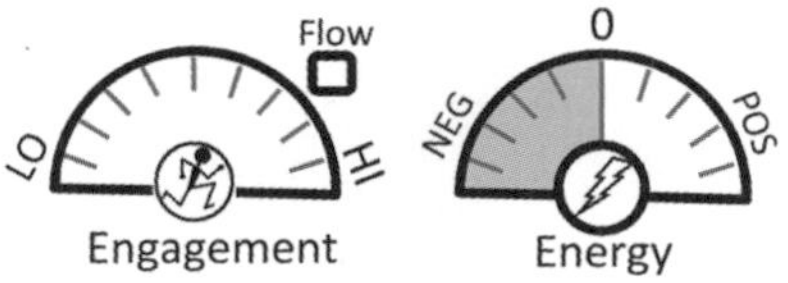

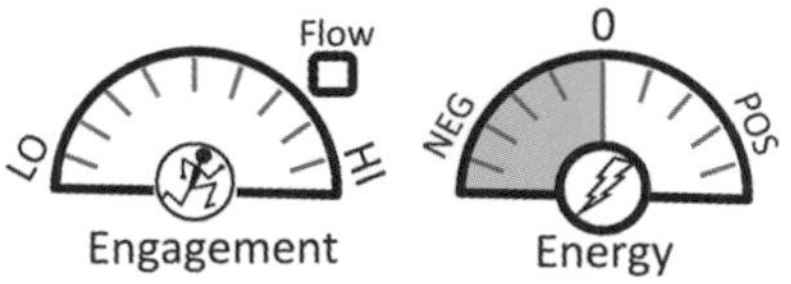

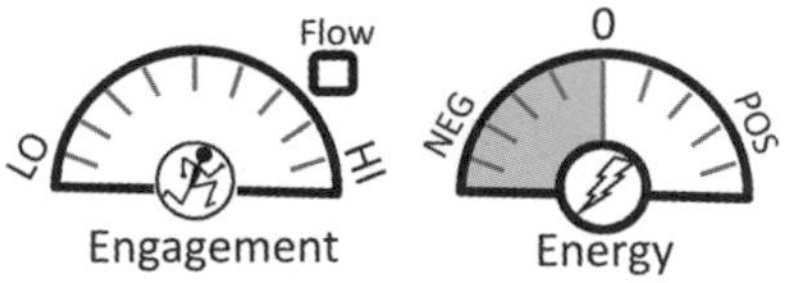

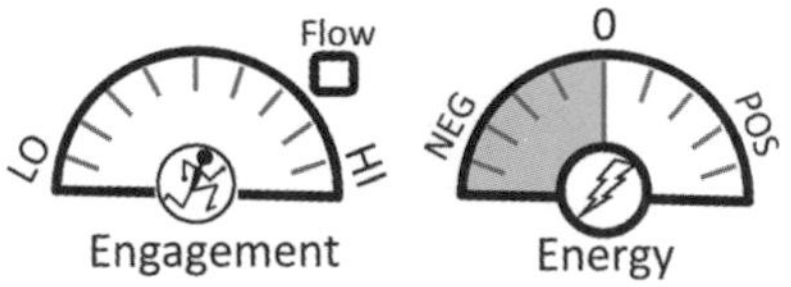

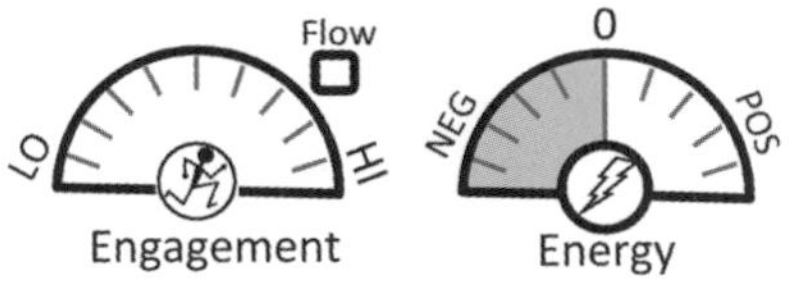

Which activities flowed effortlessly for you? (See page 48 for a description of "flow.")

_____

_____

_____

_____

_____

_____

Which activities left you with more energy than you had at the start?

_____

_____

_____

_____

_____

_____

Which activities drained energy from you?

_____

_____

_____

_____

_____

_____

FOLLOW
WHAT
ENGAGES
AND
EXCITES YOU,
WHAT
BRINGS YOU
ALIVE.

Date: _____

_____

_____

_____

_____

_____

_____

_____

_____

_____

_____

_____

_____

_____

_____

_____

_____

_____

_____

_____

_____

_____

_____

_____

Engagement   Energy

Engagement   Energy

Engagement   Energy

Engagement   Energy

Engagement   Energy

Engagement   Energy

Engagement   Energy

Engagement   Energy

Date: _____

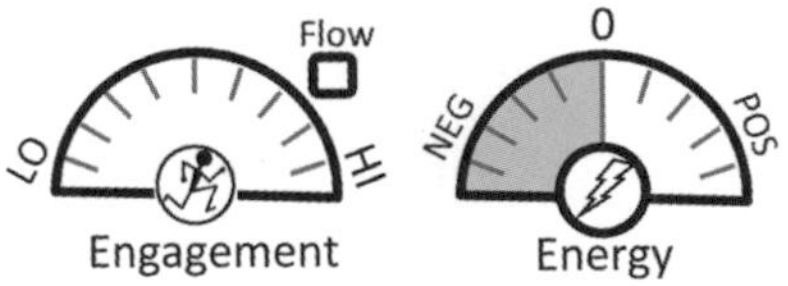

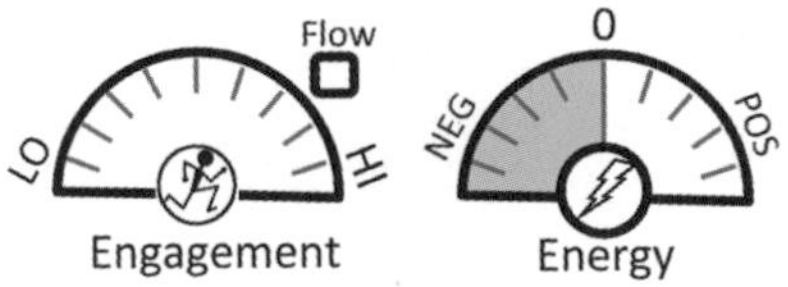

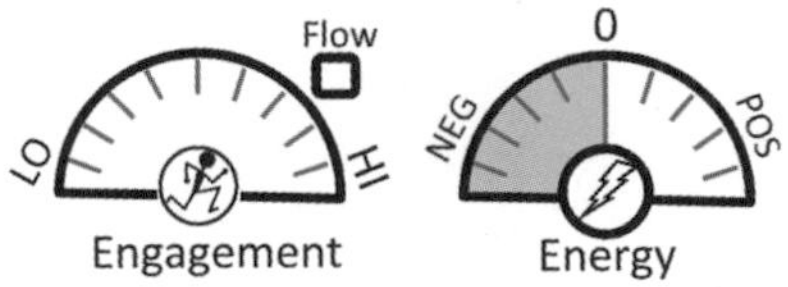

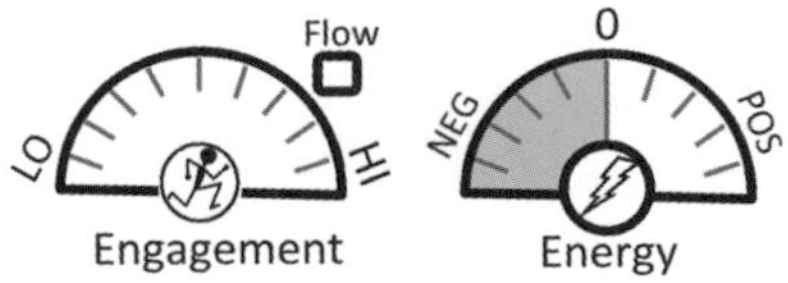

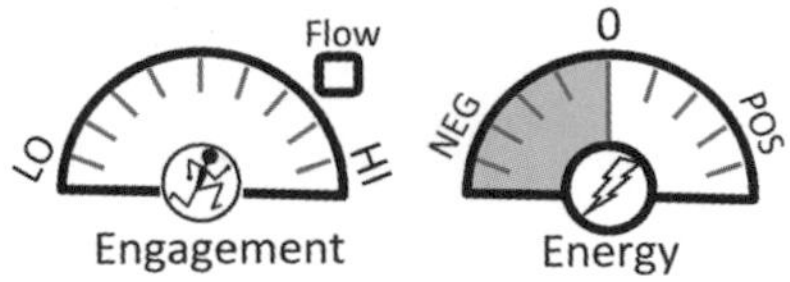

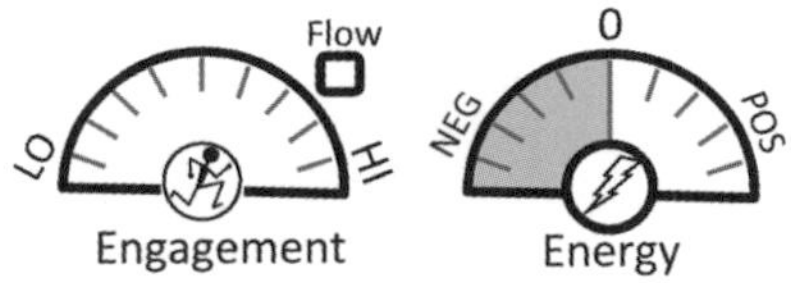

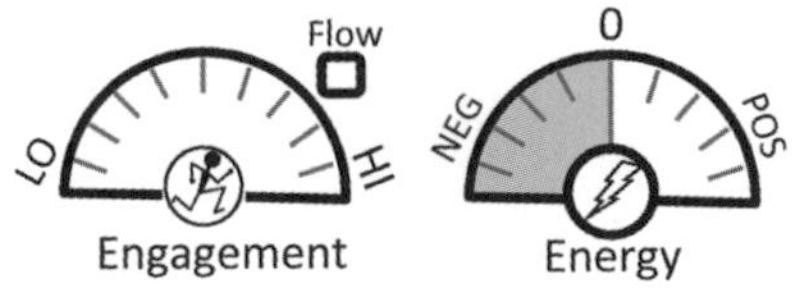

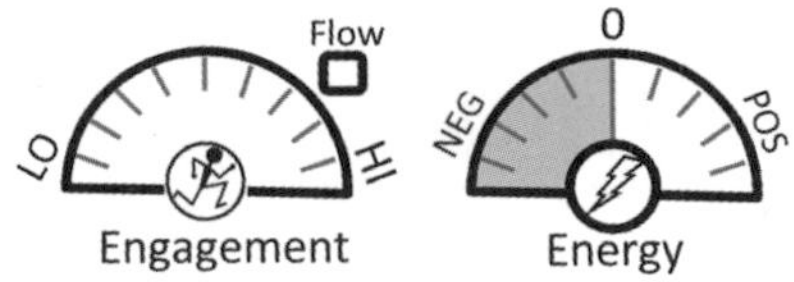

_____

_____

_____

_____

_____

_____

_____

_____

_____

_____

_____

_____

_____

_____

_____

_____

_____

_____

_____

_____

_____

_____

Date: _____

_____

_____

_____

Flow ☐
LO | HI — Engagement
0 — NEG POS — Energy

_____

_____

_____

Flow ☐
LO | HI — Engagement
0 — NEG POS — Energy

_____

_____

_____

Flow ☐
LO | HI — Engagement
0 — NEG POS — Energy

_____

_____

_____

Flow ☐
LO | HI — Engagement
0 — NEG POS — Energy

_____

_____

_____

Flow ☐
LO | HI — Engagement
0 — NEG POS — Energy

_____

_____

_____

Flow ☐
LO | HI — Engagement
0 — NEG POS — Energy

_____

_____

_____

Flow ☐
LO | HI — Engagement
0 — NEG POS — Energy

_____

_____

_____

Flow ☐
LO | HI — Engagement
0 — NEG POS — Energy

Date: _____

Engagement Energy

Engagement Energy

Engagement Energy

Engagement Energy

Engagement Energy

Engagement Energy

Engagement Energy

Engagement Energy

Date: _____

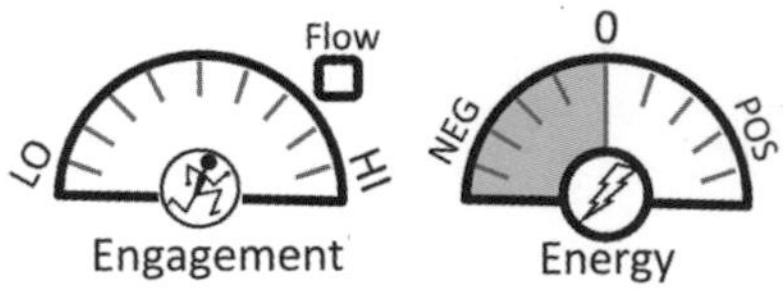

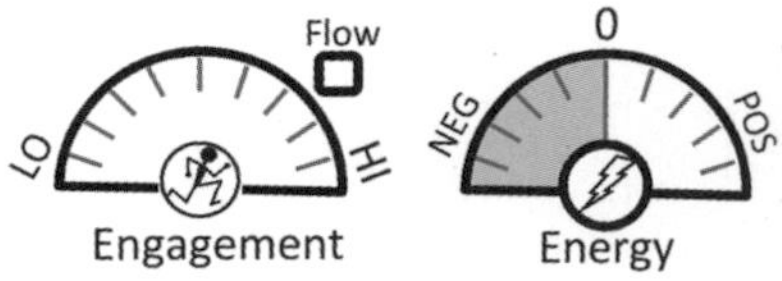

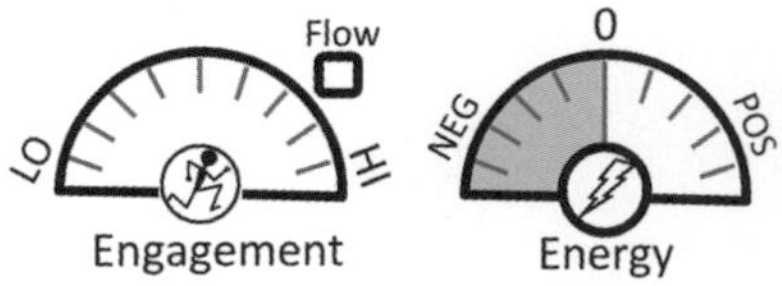

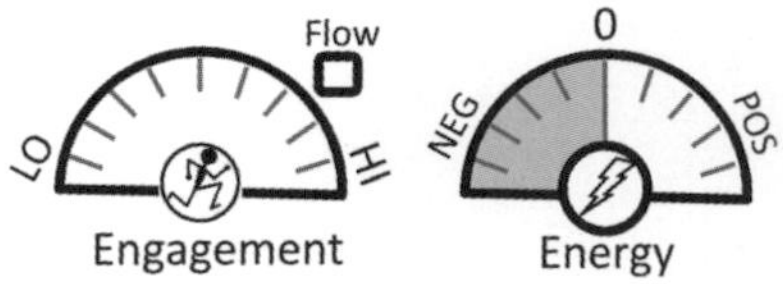

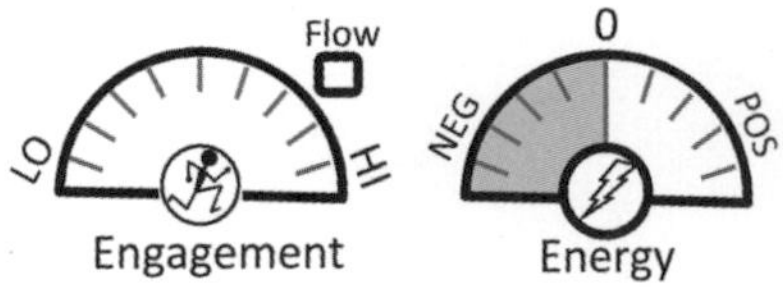

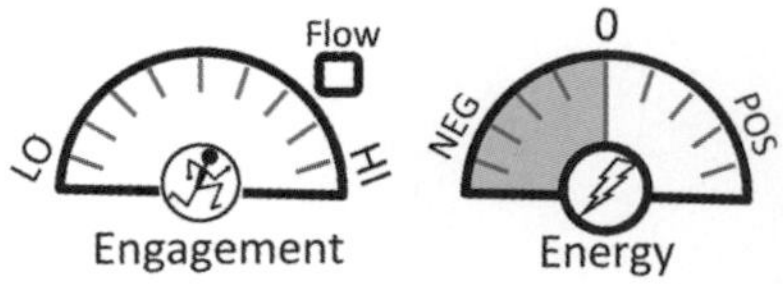

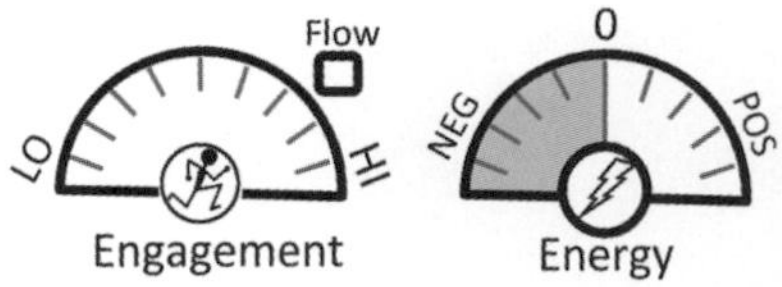

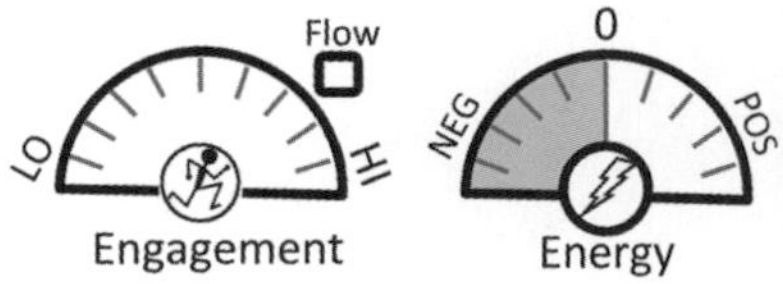

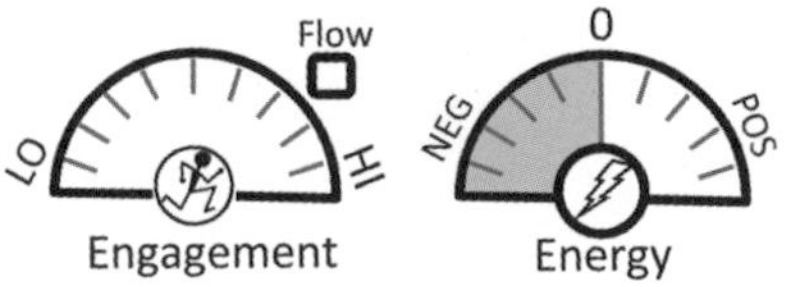

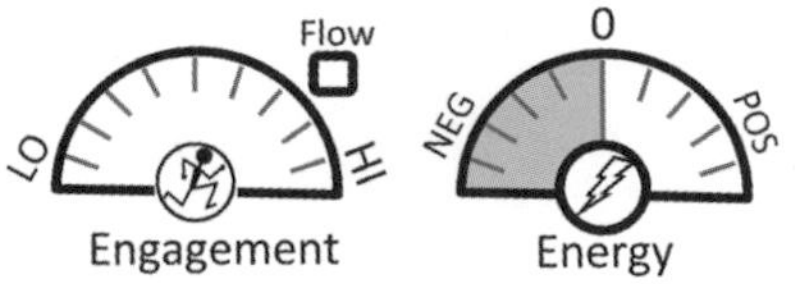

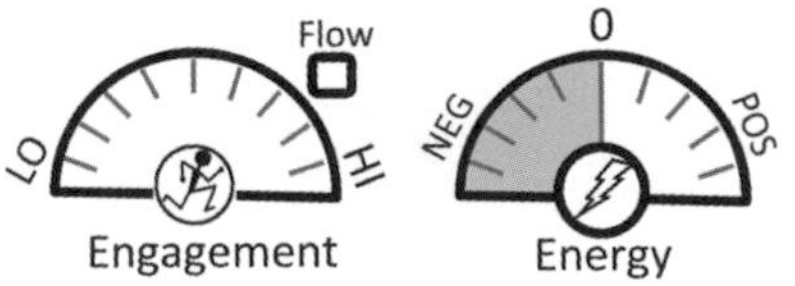

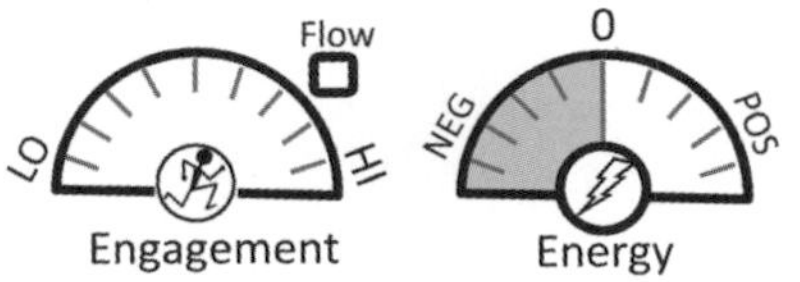

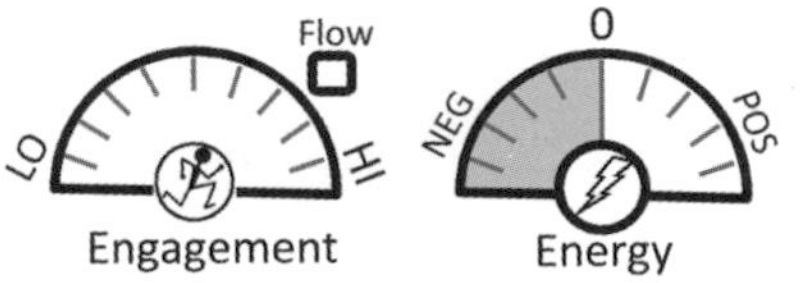

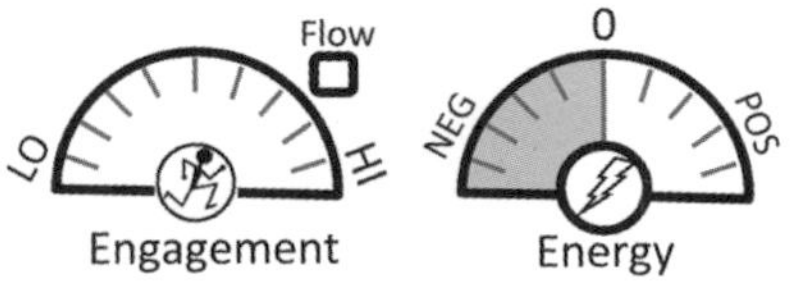

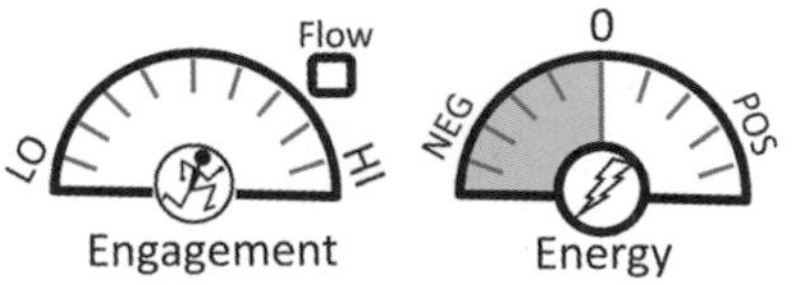

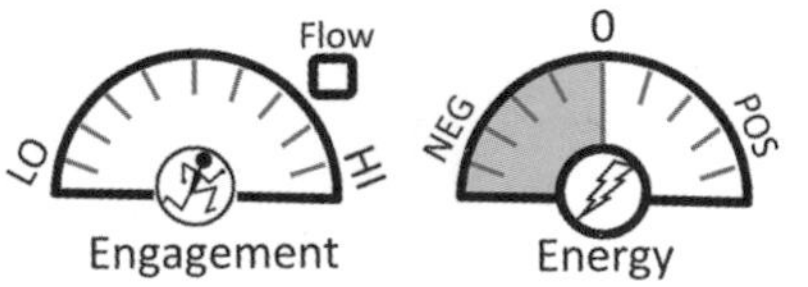

_____

_____

_____

_____

_____

_____

_____

_____

_____

_____

_____

_____

_____

_____

_____

_____

_____

_____

_____

_____

_____

_____

_____

_____

Date: _____

_____

_____

_____

Engagement · Energy

_____

_____

_____

Engagement · Energy

_____

_____

_____

Engagement · Energy

_____

_____

_____

Engagement · Energy

_____

_____

_____

Engagement · Energy

_____

_____

_____

Engagement · Energy

_____

_____

_____

Engagement · Energy

_____

_____

_____

Engagement · Energy

END-OF-WEEK REFLECTIONS

Which activities flowed effortlessly for you? (See page 48 for a description of "flow.")

_____
_____
_____
_____
_____
_____

Which activities left you with more energy than you had at the start?

_____
_____
_____
_____
_____
_____

Which activities drained energy from you?

_____
_____
_____
_____
_____
_____

Date: _____

_____
_____
_____

Flow □
LO · Engagement · HI
NEG · 0 · POS
Energy

_____
_____
_____

Flow □
LO · Engagement · HI
NEG · 0 · POS
Energy

_____
_____
_____

Flow □
LO · Engagement · HI
NEG · 0 · POS
Energy

_____
_____
_____

Flow □
LO · Engagement · HI
NEG · 0 · POS
Energy

_____
_____
_____

Flow □
LO · Engagement · HI
NEG · 0 · POS
Energy

_____
_____
_____

Flow □
LO · Engagement · HI
NEG · 0 · POS
Energy

_____
_____
_____

Flow □
LO · Engagement · HI
NEG · 0 · POS
Energy

_____
_____
_____

Flow □
LO · Engagement · HI
NEG · 0 · POS
Energy

Flow
LO / HI
Engagement

0
NEG / POS
Energy

Flow
LO / HI
Engagement

0
NEG / POS
Energy

Flow
LO / HI
Engagement

0
NEG / POS
Energy

Flow
LO / HI
Engagement

0
NEG / POS
Energy

Flow
LO / HI
Engagement

0
NEG / POS
Energy

Flow
LO / HI
Engagement

0
NEG / POS
Energy

Flow
LO / HI
Engagement

0
NEG / POS
Energy

Flow
LO / HI
Engagement

0
NEG / POS
Energy

Date: _____

_____

_____

_____

_____

_____

_____

_____

_____

_____

_____

_____

_____

_____

_____

_____

_____

_____

_____

_____

_____

_____

_____

Flow
Engagement

Energy

Flow
Engagement

Energy

Flow
Engagement

Energy

Flow
Engagement

Energy

Flow
Engagement

Energy

Flow
Engagement

Energy

Flow
Engagement

Energy

Flow
Engagement

Energy

Engagement — Energy

Engagement — Energy

Engagement — Energy

Engagement — Energy

Engagement — Energy

Engagement — Energy

Engagement — Energy

Engagement — Energy

MAXIMIZE
YOUR
VITALITY.

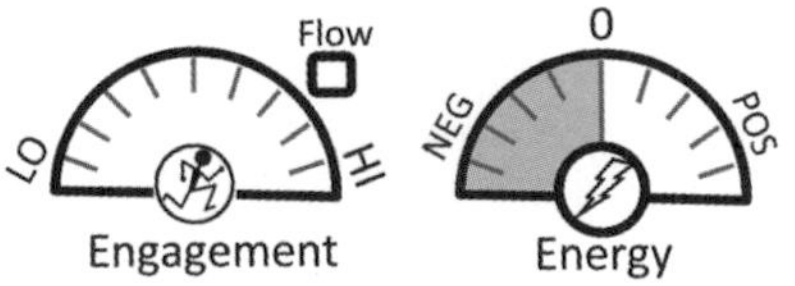

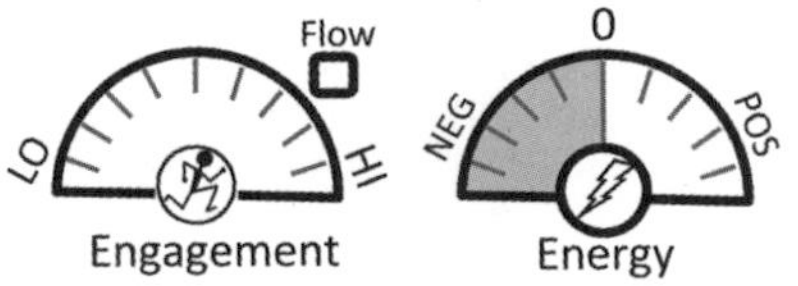

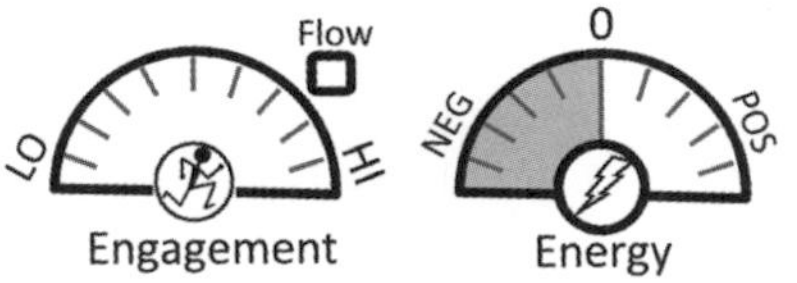

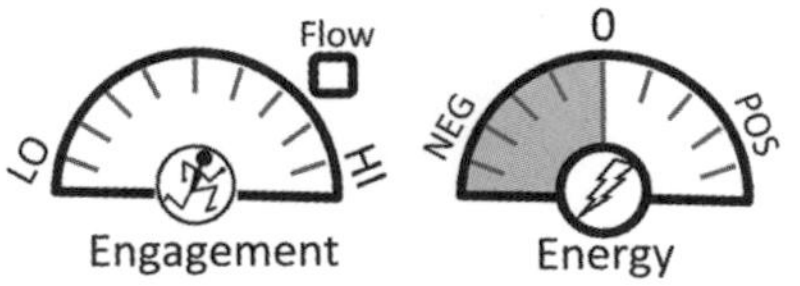

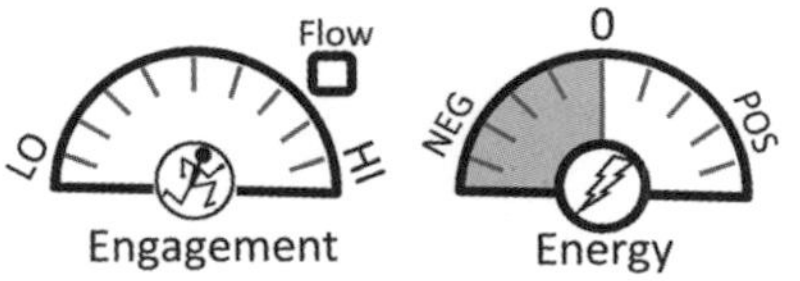

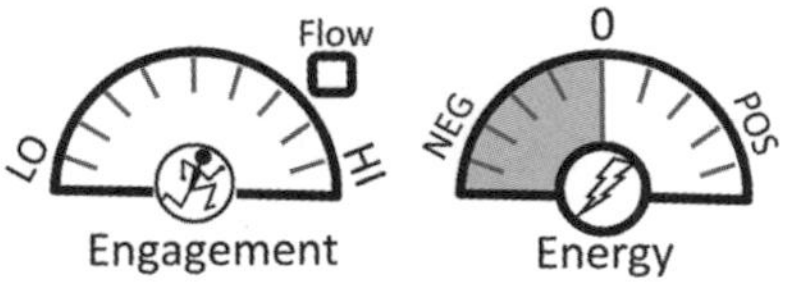

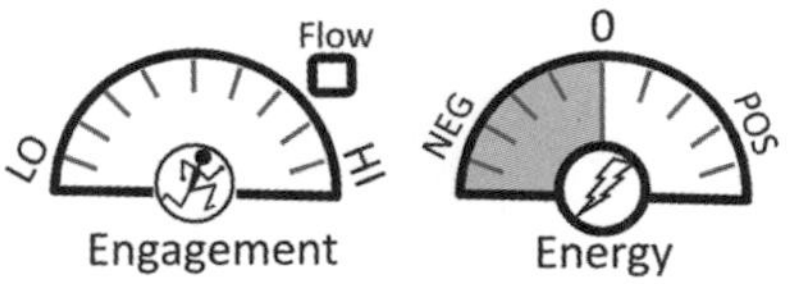

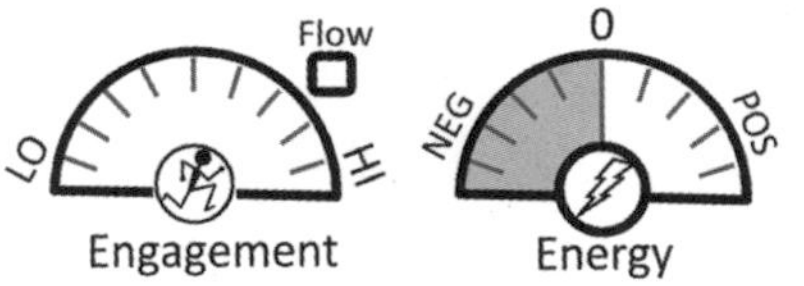

_____

_____

_____

_____

_____

_____

_____

_____

_____

_____

_____

_____

_____

_____

_____

_____

_____

_____

_____

_____

_____

_____

_____

Date: _____

_____

_____

_____

Engagement — Energy

_____

_____

_____

Engagement — Energy

_____

_____

_____

Engagement — Energy

_____

_____

_____

Engagement — Energy

_____

_____

_____

Engagement — Energy

_____

_____

_____

Engagement — Energy

_____

_____

_____

Engagement — Energy

_____

_____

_____

Engagement — Energy

Date: _____

_____

_____

_____

Engagement Energy

_____

_____

_____

Engagement Energy

_____

_____

_____

Engagement Energy

_____

_____

_____

Engagement Energy

_____

_____

_____

Engagement Energy

_____

_____

_____

Engagement Energy

_____

_____

_____

Engagement Energy

_____

_____

_____

Engagement Energy

Which activities flowed effortlessly for you? (See page 48 for a description of "flow.")

_____

_____

_____

_____

_____

_____

Which activities left you with more energy than you had at the start?

_____

_____

_____

_____

_____

_____

Which activities drained energy from you?

_____

_____

_____

_____

_____

_____

ANNOTATING YOUR GOOD TIME JOURNAL

Now let's go back through your journal pages to find the high and low points of your days— then we can dig deeper from there. Using the writing space on the following pages, note where you experience activities that engage you, produce flow, generate positive energy, or create negative energy.

Engagement

Flow

Engaged

When were you engaged—excited, focused, and having a good time? Find them in your Good Time Journal and list them here:

_____

_____

_____

_____

_____

_____

_____

_____

_____

_____

_____

_____

_____

_____

_____

_____

_____

_____

_____

_____

_____

Flow

People in flow report experiencing complete involvement in the activity, a sense of ecstasy or euphoria, great inner clarity, total calmness, or the notion that time is standing still. A really satisfying career involves a lot of flow states. Look at the places you checked off and list them here:

_____

_____

_____

_____

_____

_____

_____

_____

_____

_____

_____

_____

_____

_____

_____

_____

_____

_____

Energy

Positive and Negative Energy

Some activities sustain our energy, while others suck the life right out of us and leave us drained for whatever comes next. Note that energy and engagement are not the same thing. There may be activities that engage but also exhaust you. List them all here:

Energy-Positive Activities:

_____

_____

_____

_____

_____

_____

_____

_____

_____

_____

_____

_____

_____

_____

_____

Energy-Negative Activities:

_____

_____

_____

_____

_____

_____

_____

_____

_____

_____

_____

_____

_____

_____

_____

AEIOU:
FOCUSING ON
THE GOOD STUFF

In order to better set your wayfinding direction, you want to be as precise as possible about what's working and what's not in any given day. Look back at your journal annotations on pages 48–49 and find the activities where you were highly engaged or experiencing a flow state. Let's get even more specific about what was working during those times with the AEIOU Method.

TRY IT

On the following pages, identify four key experiences or activities that get you moving toward cloud nine, then drill down into them by answering the questions in as much detail as possible.

HIGH POINT 1

_____

Activities: What were you actually doing? Was it a structured or unstructured activity?
Were you a leader or a participant?

_____

_____

_____

Environments: What kind of place were you in? How did it make you feel?

_____

_____

_____

Interactions: Were others involved? Was your interaction formal or informal?

_____

_____

_____

Objects: Were you using any objects or devices during this activity? Which ones, if any,
kept you engaged?

_____

_____

_____

Users: Who else was there and what role did they play in your experience?

_____

_____

_____

Activities: What were you actually doing? Was it a structured or unstructured activity? Were you a leader or a participant?

_____

_____

_____

Environments: What kind of place were you in? How did it make you feel?

_____

_____

_____

Interactions: Were others involved? Was your interaction formal or informal?

_____

_____

_____

Objects: Were you using any objects or devices during this activity? Which ones, if any, kept you engaged?

_____

_____

_____

Users: Who else was there and what role did they play in your experience?

_____

_____

_____

HIGH POINT **3**

_____

Activities: What were you actually doing? Was it a structured or unstructured activity?
Were you a leader or a participant?

_____

_____

_____

Environments: What kind of place were you in? How did it make you feel?

_____

_____

_____

Interactions: Were others involved? Was your interaction formal or informal?

_____

_____

_____

Objects: Were you using any objects or devices during this activity? Which ones, if any,
kept you engaged?

_____

_____

_____

Users: Who else was there and what role did they play in your experience?

_____

_____

_____

Activities: What were you actually doing? Was it a structured or unstructured activity? Were you a leader or a participant?

_____

_____

_____

Environments: What kind of place were you in? How did it make you feel?

_____

_____

_____

Interactions: Were others involved? Was your interaction formal or informal?

_____

_____

_____

Objects: Were you using any objects or devices during this activity? Which ones, if any, kept you engaged?

_____

_____

_____

Users: Who else was there and what role did they play in your experience?

_____

_____

_____

MINING THE MOUNTAINTOP

Your previous experiences are also waiting to be mined for insights—we call these mountaintop moments, or "peak experiences," the times when you truly enjoyed yourself. Whether it's a specific initiative you led at your job, a school project you created, a summer program you joined, or a volunteer activity you loved, write a few paragraphs about these good memories that have stuck with you. Note the activities from that experience that most engaged and energized you.

AEIOU: ZOOMING IN ON THE BAD STUFF

Find areas in your Good Time Journal where you experienced low engagement and negative energy. Try to get a sense of what specifically you did not enjoy. Your focus might be nurtured or frustrated by other people, depending on the form of collaboration. For instance, perhaps you thought you didn't like working with others, but the AEIOU Method might reveal that in fact you prefer to work in small groups that focus on creative tasks, rather than attending big meetings about business strategy.

TRY IT

Just as you did with your four high points, identify at least four low points, then answer the questions on the following pages to clarify what was so bad about them.

LOW POINT 1

_____

Activities: What were you actually doing? Was it a structured or unstructured activity? Were you a leader or a participant?

_____

_____

_____

Environments: What kind of place were you in? How did it make you feel?

_____

_____

_____

Interactions: Were others involved? Was your interaction formal or informal?

_____

_____

_____

Objects: Were you using any objects or devices during this activity? Which ones, if any, were distracting or cumbersome?

_____

_____

_____

Users: Who else was there and what role did they play in your experience?

_____

_____

_____

LOW POINT _____

Activities: What were you actually doing? Was it a structured or unstructured activity? Were you a leader or a participant?

_____

_____

_____

Environments: What kind of place were you in? How did it make you feel?

_____

_____

_____

Interactions: Were others involved? Was your interaction formal or informal?

_____

_____

_____

Objects: Were you using any objects or devices during this activity? Which ones, if any, were distracting or cumbersome?

_____

_____

_____

Users: Who else was there and what role did they play in your experience?

_____

_____

_____

LOW POINT 3 _____

Activities: What were you actually doing? Was it a structured or unstructured activity? Were you a leader or a participant?

_____

_____

_____

Environments: What kind of place were you in? How did it make you feel?

_____

_____

_____

Interactions: Were others involved? Was your interaction formal or informal?

_____

_____

_____

Objects: Were you using any objects or devices during this activity? Which ones, if any, were distracting or cumbersome?

_____

_____

_____

Users: Who else was there and what role did they play in your experience?

_____

_____

_____

Activities: What were you actually doing? Was it a structured or unstructured activity? Were you a leader or a participant?

_____

_____

_____

Environments: What kind of place were you in? How did it make you feel?

_____

_____

_____

Interactions: Were others involved? Was your interaction formal or informal?

_____

_____

_____

Objects: Were you using any objects or devices during this activity? Which ones, if any, were distracting or cumbersome?

_____

_____

_____

Users: Who else was there and what role did they play in your experience?

_____

_____

_____

Armed with your compass and your Good Time Journal
insights, you can now do a great job of wayfinding
without knowing your exact destination.

LIKE
Lewis & Clark,
YOU ARE STARTING TO MAP SOME OF THE TERRITORY YOU'VE COVERED, AND TO SEE NEW POSSIBILITIES IN THE TERRITORY AHEAD.

GETTING UNSTUCK

We are all stuck in some areas of our lives. That's where ideation comes into play, which is just a fancy word for coming up with lots of ideas. To move past obstacles, you need to generate more ideas and options than you ever thought possible, keeping in mind that you choose better when you have lots of ideas to consider. You should never choose your first solution to any problem.

Write about a time when you didn't feel self-conscious about being creative—even if it was when you were a young child. What did it feel like to draw without judgment, or to sing without worrying how you sounded? Try to remember the experience of creating just for the fun of it. How can you reconnect with that energy?

_____

_____

_____

_____

_____

_____

_____

_____

_____

_____

_____

_____

_____

_____

_____

_____

_____

_____

_____

_____

_____

MIND MAPPING

In order to get your intuition flowing and generate ideas that you can start testing out, use this ideation technique. The activity of mind mapping combines simple free association of words (which uses one side of your brain) with drawing on paper (which uses another side of your brain). The result: dozens of concepts you never thought possible. Because this technique is a visual method and meant to be done rapidly, it bypasses your inner logical/verbal censor.

Pick a topic: Look back at your Good Time Journal (pages 20–49) and choose an activity that engaged you, generated positive energy, or created a flow state. Try to articulate the essence of the activity in one or two words to create your mind map topic. Write it in the center of a large piece of paper and circle it.

Make a mind map: Take three to five minutes to write down five or six things related to your topic, jotting down the *first* things that come to mind, then circling them. Don't overthink it and don't judge. Repeat step two by writing down words in a second ring that are related to the first. Do this again by drawing three or four lines from each peripheral word and jotting down even more related ideas (they do not have to be related to your central topic or your first ring). Keep going until you have at least three or four rings of word associations.

Create mash-ups: Choosing from the outer ring of your random associations, highlight ideas that are interesting or jump out at you. They do not have to be related. Try combining these individual components into a couple of possible scenarios that you might want to test out.

ON THE FOLLOWING PAGES, YOU'LL BE PROMPTED TO CREATE MIND MAPS ON THE FOLD-OUT DOTTED PAPER FOR ENGAGEMENT, ENERGY, AND FLOW. THEN ON PAGE 79 YOU'LL CREATE MASH-UPS FROM THOSE MIND MAPS.

MIND MAP

ENGAGEMENT

Choose an activity from your Good Time Journal that kept you fully engaged. Express the essence of this activity in one or two words, add it to the center of the dotted paper, and create a mind map around that topic in three to five minutes.

THE
#1 enemy
OF CREATIVITY
IS JUDGMENT.

Choose an activity from your Good Time Journal that energized you. Express the essence of this activity in one or two words, add it to the center of the dotted paper, and create a mind map around that topic in three to five minutes.

STOP
TRYING TO
"GET IT RIGHT"
AND START
DESIGNING
YOUR WAY
forward.

Choose a time from your Good Time Journal when you experienced flow. Express the essence of this activity in one or two words, add it to the center of the dotted paper, and create a mind map around that topic in three to five minutes.

DESIGNERS
KNOW
THAT YOU
never go with
YOUR FIRST
IDEA.

MIND
MAP
MASH-UPS

Now that you've done these mind maps, you're going to select a few random ideas and combine them in ways you'd never expect. Then try imagining an interesting—though not necessarily practical—life alternative from each. Defer judgment and quiet your internal critic while you ideate.

ENGAGEMENT MASH-UP

Look at the outer ring of your Engagement Mind Map and pick three disparate items that catch your eye. (You'll know which ones they are intuitively. Look for the ones that start to "jump out" at you.)

1. _____

2. _____

3. _____

Try to combine these three items into a possible job that would be fun for you and helpful for someone else. (Again, it need not be practical.) Give the position a title, a description, and then draw a quick napkin sketch of what this new job looks like.

Job Title: _____

Description: _____

_____

Napkin Sketch:

ACCEPT THE
PROBLEM.
GET STUCK.
GET OVER IT
AND IDEATE!

Look at the outer ring of your Energy Mind Map and write down three disparate items that catch your eye:

1. _____

2. _____

3. _____

Try to combine these three items into a possible job that would be fun for you and helpful for someone else. (Again, it need not be practical.) Give the position a title, a description, and then draw a quick napkin sketch of what this new job looks like.

Job Title: _____

Description: _____

_____

Napkin Sketch:

Look at the outer ring of your Flow Mind Map and write down three disparate items that catch your eye:

1. _____

2. _____

3. _____

Try to combine these three items into a possible job that would be fun for you and helpful for someone else. (Again, it need not be practical.) Give the position a title, a description, and then draw a quick napkin sketch of what this new job looks like.

Job Title: _____

Description: _____

_____

Napkin Sketch:

LIFE DESIGN
IS ABOUT
GENERATING
OPTIONS.

CREATING ODYSSEY PLANS

There are lots of true, coherent, interesting, and different versions of each person, so rather than designing one *life*, we invite you to design many *lives* and imagine multiple ways you could launch the next chapter of your life's quest. We call these Odyssey Plans: sketches of viable and substantially different possibilities that animate your imagination and allow you to make better choices. Even if you're not looking to make a change from your One True Plan, you still need to develop parallel options so you don't get stuck trying to refine the same plan over and over again.

1. A visual/graphic time line of a five-year career plan that includes non-career bucket list events as well (year one below includes bartending school and a personal yoga practice)

2. A short headline describing the Odyssey Plan

3. Two to three questions the life alternative addresses. These are not questions about the plan but curiosities that might be satisfied by living this way for five years.

4. A dashboard that gauges:
   a. Resources (Do you have the time, money, skill, and contacts you need to pull off this plan?)
   b. Likeability (How do you feel about this plan?)
   c. Confidence (How confident are you about pulling this off?)
   d. Coherence (Is the plan consistent with your Workview and Lifeview?)

Example: "Creating Community—One Drink at a Time!"

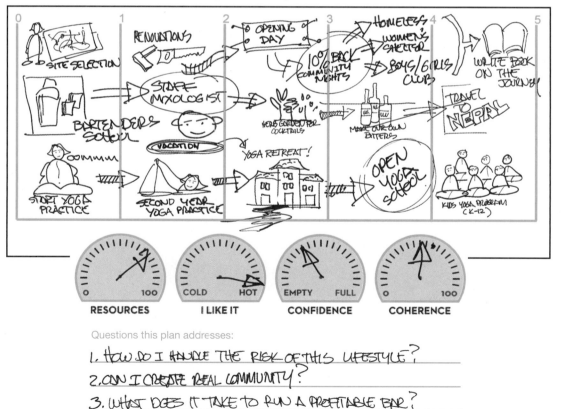

Complete three alternative five-year plans of your own, following the example on page 83 and drawing your mind map mash-ups, if you'd like.

LIFE ONE: Your current life or the idea you've been nursing for some time.

Title: _____

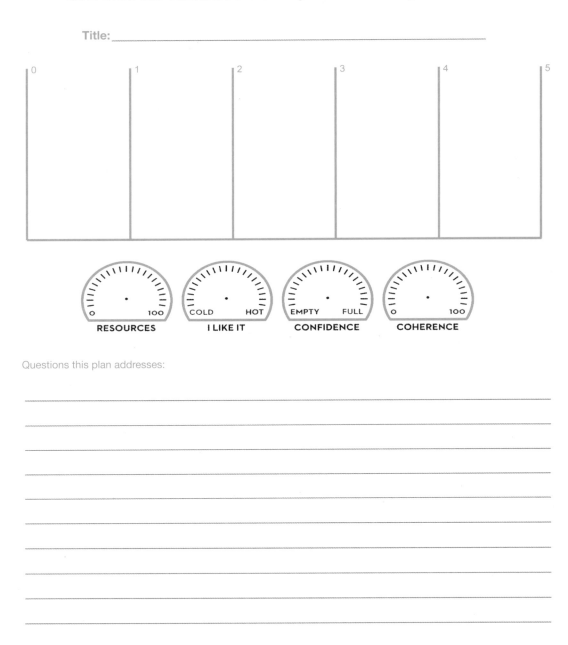

Questions this plan addresses:

_____
_____
_____
_____
_____
_____
_____
_____
_____
_____
_____

LIFE TWO: That thing you'd do if thing one were suddenly gone.

Title: _____

0	1	2	3	4	5

RESOURCES
0 — 100

I LIKE IT
COLD — HOT

CONFIDENCE
EMPTY — FULL

COHERENCE
0 — 100

Questions this plan addresses:

_____
_____
_____
_____
_____
_____
_____
_____
_____
_____

LIFE THREE: The thing you'd do or life you'd live if money were no object.

Title: _____

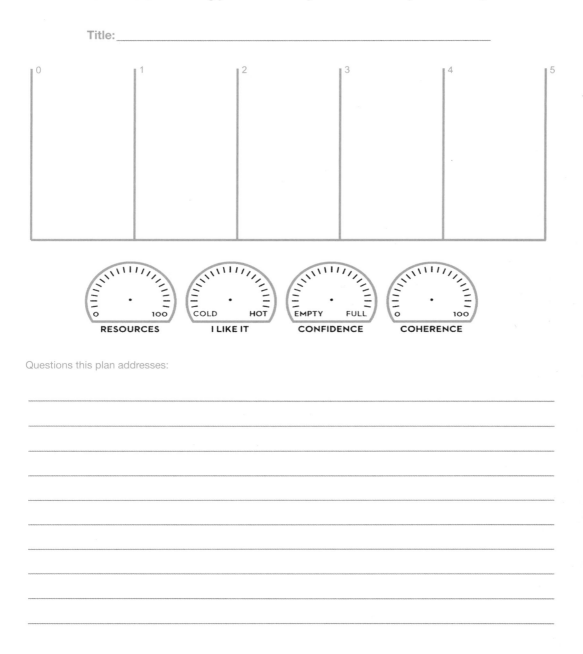

0   1   2   3   4   5

RESOURCES	I LIKE IT	CONFIDENCE	COHERENCE
0 — 100	COLD — HOT	EMPTY — FULL	0 — 100

Questions this plan addresses:

_____

_____

_____

_____

_____

_____

_____

_____

_____

_____

REFLECT ON YOUR PLANS

The best way to interact with your alternatives is to share them aloud with a group of friends. You want to choose people who will ask good questions but not offer critique or unwanted advice. Use these pages to keep track of notes and questions that come up when you present your three Odyssey Plans. Here are some questions to reflect on:

Which plan excites you the most?

_____

_____

_____

_____

_____

Which plan feels draining?

_____

_____

_____

_____

_____

Which plan plays it safe? Which is risky?

_____

_____

_____

_____

_____

What do you notice as you reflect on and compare your dashboards? Are any preference criteria becoming clear to you?

_____

_____

_____

_____

What questions do you have about taking any of these paths?

_____

_____

_____

_____

_____

How might you prototype or test out one of these experiences to understand it better?

_____

_____

_____

_____

_____

FRAMING A GOOD QUESTION

Free-associating with others will generate energy and momentum toward exploring your Odyssey Plans and other goals. Convene at least three to six people who are willing to bounce ideas around. Give everyone an open-ended question about one of your Odyssey Plans to focus your brainstorm. You might ask the group, "What are the functions of this potential path or career?" Or, "How many ways can I take action to learn more about this path before I make the leap?" Use the following pages to capture the results.

RULES
OF
BRAINSTORMING

1

Go for quantity, not quality.

2

Defer judgment and do not censor ideas.

3

Build off the ideas of others.

4

Encourage wild ideas.

BRAINSTORM 1

Date: _____

Question: _____

_____

Notes: _____

_____

_____

_____

_____

_____

_____

_____

_____

_____

_____

_____

_____

_____

_____

_____

_____

_____

_____

_____

_____

_____

_____

_____

_____

_____

_____

NAMING AND FRAMING THE OUTCOME

After your brainstorming session, process your material by answering the following questions.

How many ideas did you come up with?

_____

_____

_____

_____

_____

_____

Which two were the most exciting?

_____

_____

_____

_____

_____

_____

Which one would you do if money were no object?

_____

_____

_____

_____

_____

_____

Which one probably won't work, but if it did you'd be thrilled?

_____

_____

_____

_____

_____

_____

Which ideas made the final cut?

_____

_____

_____

_____

_____

_____

What's the one idea you want to tackle first? Second?

_____

_____

_____

_____

_____

_____

BRAINSTORM 2

Date: _____

Question: _____

_____

Notes: _____

_____

_____

_____

_____

_____

_____

_____

_____

_____

_____

_____

_____

_____

_____

_____

_____

_____

_____

_____

_____

_____

_____

_____

_____

_____

_____

_____

_____

After your brainstorming session, process your material by answering
the following questions.

How many ideas did you come up with?

_____

_____

_____

_____

_____

Which two were the most exciting?

_____

_____

_____

_____

_____

**Which one would you do if money were
no object?**

_____

_____

_____

_____

_____

**Which one probably won't work, but if it did
you'd be thrilled?**

_____

_____

_____

_____

_____

Which ideas made the final cut?

_____

_____

_____

_____

_____

**What's the one idea you want to tackle
first? Second?**

_____

_____

_____

_____

_____

BRAINSTORM 3

Date: _____

Question: _____
_____

Notes: _____
_____
_____
_____
_____
_____
_____
_____
_____
_____
_____
_____
_____
_____
_____
_____
_____
_____
_____
_____
_____
_____
_____
_____
_____
_____

NAMING AND FRAMING THE OUTCOME

After your brainstorming session, process your material by answering
the following questions.

How many ideas did you come up with?

_____

_____

_____

_____

_____

_____

Which two were the most exciting?

_____

_____

_____

_____

_____

_____

Which one would you do if money were
no object?

_____

_____

_____

_____

_____

_____

Which one probably won't work, but if it did
you'd be thrilled?

_____

_____

_____

_____

_____

_____

Which ideas made the final cut?

_____

_____

_____

_____

_____

_____

What's the one idea you want to tackle
first? Second?

_____

_____

_____

_____

_____

_____

If you're overwhelmed by all the options you've generated, the key is to reframe your ideas by realizing that if you have too many, you actually have none at all. Options only create value in your life when they are chosen and realized.

TRY IT

Choose twelve options from your brainstorms on pages 90–95. List them below.

1. _____
2. _____
3. _____
4. _____
5. _____
6. _____
7. _____
8. _____
9. _____
10. _____
11. _____
12. _____

Eliminate seven options that don't fit your identity by taking into consideration your Workview and Lifeview and Odyssey Plans. Rewrite the remaining five here.

1. _____
2. _____
3. _____
4. _____
5. _____

Now you have a can't-lose situation on your hands. All five options are strategically worthwhile, which leaves you to choose based on secondary considerations (easier commute, better storytelling potential).

ONLY BY
TAKING ACTION
CAN WE BUILD
OUR WAY
forward.

PROTOTYPING YOUR PLANS

Designers have a bias to action. By doing small experiments, meeting people, and exploring your options through hands-on experience you'll get a lot further than by only reading, thinking, and reflecting. We call this physical experience in the world "prototyping."

Examples of prototyping include:

1. Conversations with people doing something you might like to do (a Life Design Interview)

2. Shadowing professionals you'd like to emulate

3. One-week unpaid exploratory project that you create

4. A three-month internship

5. A scaled-down version of the career you envision (for example, catering instead of opening a restaurant)

What other experiences might help you? Add them to the list.

6. _____

7. _____

8. _____

LIFE DESIGN CONVERSATION TRACKER

Find someone doing or living one or more of the plans you're contemplating, and ask them to have a conversation. Keep track of all of your Life Design conversations on the following pages.

Contact name: _____

Company: _____

Date contacted: _____

Response: _____

Meeting date: _____

Conversation notes: _____

_____

_____

_____

_____

_____

_____

_____

_____

_____

_____

_____

_____

_____

CONVERSATION 2

Contact name: _____

Company: _____

Date contacted: _____

Response: _____

Meeting date: _____

Conversation notes: _____

_____

_____

_____

_____

_____

_____

_____

_____

_____

_____

_____

_____

_____

WE PROTOTYPE TO
ASK *good questions*,
CREATE EXPERIENCES,
REVEAL OUR ASSUMPTIONS,
FAIL FAST, *fail forward*,
SNEAK UP ON THE FUTURE,
AND *build empathy* FOR
OURSELVES AND OTHERS.

Contact name: _____

Company: _____

Date contacted: _____

Response: _____

Meeting date: _____

Conversation notes: _____

_____

_____

_____

_____

_____

_____

_____

_____

_____

_____

_____

_____

_____

_____

Contact name: _____

Company: _____

Date contacted: _____

Response: _____

Meeting date: _____

Conversation notes: _____

_____

_____

_____

_____

_____

_____

_____

_____

_____

_____

_____

_____

_____

_____

_____

Contact name: _____

Company: _____

Date contacted: _____

Response: _____

Meeting date: _____

Conversation notes: _____

_____

_____

_____

_____

_____

_____

_____

_____

_____

_____

_____

_____

_____

_____

Contact name: _____

Company: _____

Date contacted: _____

Response: _____

Meeting date: _____

Conversation notes: _____

_____

_____

_____

_____

_____

_____

_____

_____

_____

_____

_____

_____

_____

Contact name: _____

Company: _____

Date contacted: _____

Response: _____

Meeting date: _____

Conversation notes: _____

_____

_____

_____

_____

_____

_____

_____

_____

_____

_____

_____

_____

_____

_____

Contact name: _____

Company: _____

Date contacted: _____

Response: _____

Meeting date: _____

Conversation notes: _____

_____

_____

_____

_____

_____

_____

_____

_____

_____

_____

_____

_____

_____

GOOD CHOOSING:
LET GO AND
MOVE ON

Once you've made an important decision, however big or small, you will want to make sure you implement that decision successfully by letting go and moving on. Here's an exercise to help with that very difficult and all-important last step of the choosing process. In Life Design, we know there are countless possibilities but we aren't stymied by that fact. When in doubt, let go of unnecessary options and move on, embracing your choice fully so that you can get the most from it.

EMBRACING YOUR CHOICE

You often hear people unhappily say, "Well it seemed like a good idea at the time," but of course they mean just the opposite. Often it's actually true, i.e., it was a good idea—it just didn't work out for reasons that could not have been foreseen. Too many people experience unnecessary regret for lack of clear decision awareness. By doing the reflection below, you are documenting now why this is a good decision at this time. Knowing this is valuable today and tomorrow. Set yourself up to win by reflecting and remembering!

Why did you make this particular choice?

_____

_____

_____

_____

_____

_____

_____

What engaging activities drew you to this path?

_____

_____

_____

_____

_____

_____

_____

What difficulties did you anticipate experiencing?

_____

_____

_____

_____

_____

_____

_____

How can you direct energy into enjoying the decisions you've made?

_____

_____

_____

_____

_____

_____

_____

NO MORE HAMSTER WHEEL

Designers don't spin their wheels dreaming about what could have been. They don't waste their futures by hoping for a better past. What are three ways you can commit to getting off the hamster wheel and choosing happiness instead? Write them down below.

1

2

3

FAILURE
IS JUST THE
raw material
FOR SUCCESS.

You're going to experience missteps, so it's important to understand what it means in the Life Design process: You can't fail; you can only progress and learn. Here is a simple exercise to help you reframe your flops on the way to gaining what we call "failure immunity."

TRY IT

Look back over the past two weeks. Where did you mess up? List your "failures" (F) in this log, then sort them by checking off one of three types: screwups (S), weaknesses (W), and growth opportunities (GO). Finally, capture any insights (I) to help change things next time (see example row).

F	S	W	GO	I
PHONE SURPRISE			X	START THE CALL WITH NEEDS & AGENDA

NOT ALL FAILURES ARE ALIKE

SCREWUPS =

Simple mistakes you made that you normally get right. You don't need to learn anything here; just apologize as needed and move on.

WEAKNESSES =

Mistakes you make over and over again because of one of your abiding shortcomings. Your best strategy is to avoid situations that prompt them.

GROWTH OPPORTUNITIES =

Failures that have an identifiable cause and an available solution. We want to direct our attention to this type of failure.

INSIGHTS =

Lessons you learn for real improvement. What went wrong (the critical failure factor), and what could be done differently next time (the critical success factor)?

BUILDING YOUR TEAM

All great design results from great collaboration; thinking that you alone are responsible for your life design is a misconception. Once you join a community of participants—interested friends, colleagues, or family members—you'll find more success with your life design. After all, this isn't just about you; your life design will touch many different people.

Think about the people you interacted with when discussing your Lifeview and Workview or those you identified in your Good Time Journal (20–46) who are involved in your energy-positive activities. Categorize them into Supporters, Players, and Intimates.

Supporters are those close enough to you that their encouragement helps keep you going and their feedback is of real use. Some supporters may be your friends, but not all friends are supporters, and some supporters are not friends.

The Supporters in your life include:

1. _____

2. _____

3. _____

4. _____

5. _____

Players are the active participants in your life design projects—especially your ongoing work-related and avocational projects and prototypes. These are the people you actually do things with, your coworkers in the classic sense.

The Players in your life include:

1. _____

2. _____

3. _____

4. _____

5. _____

Intimates include your immediate and close extended family members and your dearest friends. These are likely the people most directly affected by your life design.

The Intimates in your life include:

1. _____

2. _____

3. _____

4. _____

5. _____

Community IS MORE THAN JUST SHARING RESOURCES OR HANGING OUT NOW AND THEN. IT'S SHOWING UP AND *investing in the ongoing creation* OF ONE ANOTHER'S LIVES.

The three to five people who you think will be most actively engaged in designing their own lives, include:

1. _____

2. _____

3. _____

4. _____

5. _____

Tips for setting up your Life Design Team:

- If you are not yet connected to and in conversation with all of these people—get going.

- Keep an ask-for-help journal (see pages 122–142) in which you jot down the questions you want help on, and keep it handy. Each week, identify some people who can help you with some of the journal entries and reach out to them. Journal about answers and results from your helpers.

- Make sure everyone has a copy of *Designing Your Life* (or give everyone a copy), so all the members of your team understand how Life Design works and have reviewed the team roles and rules.

- Agree to meet regularly and actively to co-create a well-designed life as a community.

TRUSTING YOUR INNER VOICE

We don't always need more information to make a good decision; we also need access to that wisdom center where our well-informed emotional knowing can help us discern the better choices for us. One path to enhanced perception is to organize your thoughts in a quiet space through journaling. These last pages offer plenty of writing space to help you access a Life Design mind-set through a daily writing practice.

Unlike the Good Time Journal, where you were given specific instructions as to what to record, these blank pages are meant to capture anything you want. Use the questions below as jumping-off points for journal entries. Feel free to ask and answer your own questions, too.

1

How has your perspective changed since you began designing your life?

2

What would you like to know more about and who can help you?

3

What personal practices (such as creative or spiritual ones) can you adopt to educate your emotions and mature your discernment?

4

What are your next steps?

5

And, finally, how's it going?

Date: _____

Date: _____

Date: _____

Date: _____

Date: _____

MOST LIFE DESIGN WORK
IS DIRECTED AT *tuning up*
AND *improving the life*
you're in, WITHOUT HAVING
TO MAKE HUGE STRUCTURAL
CHANGES LIKE CHANGING
JOBS OR MOVING OR GOING
TO GRAD SCHOOL.

Date: _____

Date: _____

Date: _____

Date: _____

Date: _____

Date: _____

Date: _____

Date: _____

Date: _____

Date: _____

Date: _____

Date: _____

Date: _____

IT'S IMPOSSIBLE TO
PREDICT THE FUTURE,
BUT ONCE YOU
DESIGN SOMETHING,
it changes the future
THAT IS POSSIBLE.

BILL BURNETT is the executive director of the Design
Program at Stanford and marketing leader of the original
Apple PowerBook.

DAVE EVANS is a lecturer in the Product Design
Program at Stanford, a management consultant, and
a cofounder of Electronic Arts.

designingyour.life

Copyright © 2016, 2018 by William Burnett and David J. Evans

All rights reserved.

Published in the United States by Clarkson Potter/Publishers,
an imprint of the Crown Publishing Group, a division of Penguin
Random House LLC, New York.

crownpublishing.com
clarksonpotter.com

CLARKSON POTTER is a trademark and POTTER with colophon
is a registered trademark of Penguin Random House LLC.

Select material originally appeared in *Designing Your Life*, by
William Burnett and David J. Evans, published by Alfred A. Knopf,
a division of Penguin Random House LLC, New York, in 2016.

ISBN 978-1-5247-6181-3

Printed in China
Book design by Marysarah Quinn & Jessie Kaye
Cover design by Jessie Kaye
Edited by Rachel Federman
11
First Edition